Beauty of

Oregon

Beauty of
Oregon

Text: Paul M. Lewis
Concept & Design: Robert D. Shangle

First Printing January, 1989
Published by LTA Publishing Company
1425 S.E. 18th Avenue, Portland, Oregon 97214
Robert D. Shangle, Publisher

"Learn about America in a beautiful way."

Library of Congress Cataloging-in-Publication Data
Beauty of Oregon
/text, Paul M. Lewis; concept & design, Robert D. Shangle.
      p.   cm.
ISBN 0-917630-66-1; $19.95. — ISBN 0-917630-65-3 (pbk.); $9.95
   1. Oregon — Description and travel — 1981 — Views. I. Shangle,
Robert D. II. Title.
F877.L47   1989   88-37212
917.95'0443 — dc19   CIP

Contents

Introduction

People have a great need to know there are still places on this earth that can be called wilderness. The past few decades have brought us to an encouraging level of awareness as to the havoc man's careless technological reach has caused in formerly unspoiled areas of the world. To a greater degree than ever before, we are becoming concerned that an excessive sense of self-importance and consequent distortion of our role in the natural order may be dangerous to our health. We are able, at least, to see the danger to ourselves in continuing to be the wastrels and despoilers of the world's resources. As we begin to turn away from exploitation to conservation, our attention focuses on the task of preserving some of the wild places still remaining, those magical Shangri-las that rejuvenate the spirit.

It is important that there still be such places in the world, where nature has been allowed to hold on to some of her secrets. Deep in the wilderness we can momentarily transcend our own limitations. In the earth's wild sanctuaries, we can reach out and stretch our souls. There is some difficulty, however, in doing this while visiting some of the country's more popular wildernesses, where such activity is impeded by too many souls trying to do the same thing. The experience of nature requires a measure of solitude. The hideaways where this is possible are no longer so easy to find.

Oregon is still one of the privileged places with vast, empty, silent spaces, beautiful and remote. But there is some concern that before very long things may be a bit different. A lot of people have been finding out that Oregon is a good place to live. During the past 20 years, the rapid growth of western Oregon towns and cities has brought air and water pollution problems to the valleys that would not have been thought possible a few years earlier. Traffic congestion and urban sprawl are beginning to have a degrading effect on the quality of life in some Willamette Valley centers of population.

If Oregon's reputation for leadership and innovative approaches in environmental matters has any validity at all, it will find ways to keep its "people places" clean and beautiful and its open spaces wild and free. What makes Oregonians so ready and willing to do extraordinary things to safeguard their environment? It must be the setting itself, so beautiful in so many different ways; it seems to demand a stewardship from those who are fortunate enough to live within it.

If scenic variety stirs the esthetic sense, Oregon is well equipped to do this. It is a state of vivid contrasts, dictated by the two main natural systems that control Oregon's land, skies, and waters; the Pacific Ocean and the Cascade Range. The Cascades act as a north-to-south barrier that captures the powerful Pacific storm systems and directs most of their rain into the western valleys. The weakened cloud systems that get past the Cascade sentinels have little moisture left for the land east of the mountains.

The rain that falls blessedly and abundantly on western Oregon has occasioned, at times, some corner-of-the-mouth comments by a few trans-planted transgressors who unaccountably object to being rain-dampened when they go for a swim in a lake or the ocean. Oregon rain is both symbol and source of the generation of living things. Without so much of it, the descriptive, "spectacular," could not be applied to the wild rivers with their abundant fish life, the endless forests of fir and pine, the dazzling and pervasive green ambience of even the urban areas. Oregon's rain is nearly always gentle. Its caress can magically release the sweet forest aromas when the spell of a dry summer is first broken. Standing in a cedar grove just recently visited by rain, a forest visitor breathes a scent whose fragrant mix remains long afterwards in his memory.

The rainy third of Oregon is well known. But across the mountains the land is higher and drier, in addition to being less publicized. This region provides a startling contrast to the western part in appearance and way of life, and, of course, geological history. The southeastern section is, predominantly, a

8

desert, with ghost towns and bizarre rock formations. In this fossil-rich area, history is measured in non-human terms.

In pointing out that Oregonians are aware of what they have and are bent on preserving it, I don't wish to imply that such an attitude is their exclusive property. I think the claim can be made without belittling any other region or its people. Whether by happy accident or for some other reason, Oregon has got this far into the 20th century having escaped most of the grievous environmental injury that has been visited upon other parts of the United States and the world.

Up to very recent times, it seems to have been self-evident that whatever man *can* do, he *will* do. And since our talent for getting things done seems to have outstripped our judgmental capacities, the world around us has paid a great price for our pride of accomplishment. But Oregon is a state where consequences are measured, and we have thought a lot about the general health of the place where we are temporarily encamped. On the pages that follow, you will see symbolic evidence of how well Oregonians have succeeded in preserving the fragile beauty surrounding them. The magnificent color interpretations of several photographic artists present the many moods and faces of nature that crowd the Oregon stage.

The book also pays some attention to the works of the human participants, but these are always set against the backdrop of nature's greater drama. This is as it should be, for nearly all of Oregon's big and little towns owe their acquaintance with the good life to matchless settings provided by a prodigal nature. One brilliant example of this is found in the southern Oregon town of Ashland. There, the Oregon Shakespearean Festival, a world-famous summer celebration of the Bard, is held in an outdoor Elizabethan theatre, enfolded in an incomparable setting enhanced by man's appreciative art.

In the 1850s Theodore Winthrop (a descendant of John Winthrop of the Massachusetts Bay Colony) traveled around the Northwest and wrote about the region. It was his vision that the people of Oregon would bring the American idea to a greater realization by eliminating the worst of Old World civilization and by creating "new habits of life and thought." One might surmise with some justification that the happy relationship Oregonians are establishing with their environment is the result of those "new habits," fostered by some mysterious process of reciprocity. If Oregon remains one of the places where large areas are left in their natural state, or nearly so, it will happen because the people, here, want it that way. Having the power to do environmental good or evil, they will choose the former course, with the knowledge that their action will preserve a means of human renewal and invigoration.

P.M.L.

Northern Oregon

Oregon was, originally, the name for the Columbia, River of the West. This colossal waterway, which forms part of the border between Oregon and Washington, is now held in check by four giant dams, yet it flows with an immense power along all 1,250 miles of its length from its source, Columbia Lake in Canada. When it finally crashes into the sea just past Astoria, its energy creates whirling cross-currents that send foaming water high into the air. The Columbia is a great showoff. It gets plenty of attention from native and out-of-state admirers who ride and hike along its banks. Long ago the lordly river cut a magnificent Gorge through the Cascades for itself, the better setting to receive the homage of its human subjects, who would arrive later upon the scene.

Portland, Oregon's flagship city, gains distinction from its position on the Columbia. Situated where the river turns north and is joined by the Willamette coming up from the south, the city is an important trading cross-roads and possesses the West's largest freshwater port. A feature that makes Portland truly an Oregon city is its extensive park system. Extending through sections of the downtown area are its unique "park blocks" — complete city blocks turned over entirely to open landscaped area. In addition to these blocks, on the western hills of the city is a 5,000-acre park system that extends for nine miles and where deer and smaller wild animals find a refuge.

Portland retains its early-day flavor of lumber mills and remnants from its history of wood products manufacturing, but it is only one of a string of towns along the Columbia that have been part of the Northwest story. Some of them, downstream of Portland, are now ghost towns: first Linnton, then farther westward along the river, Fort William, Mayger, Bradwood, and Clifton. Other very much alive towns in this same stretch — like St. Helens, Scappoose, and Clatskanie — have in their midst relics of a past age, and if one drives U.S. Highway 30, which connects them, he is likely to come upon many bits of backcountry nostalgia. The Hudson's Bay Company, for example, contributed some of the residents of the Scappoose cemetery, and St. Helens' Courthouse Square is from another era. If one follows U.S. 30 all the way, he ends up, of course, at Astoria, Oregon's northernmost city, and as steeped in legend as any place in the West. Astoria watches over the last stretch of the Columbia, where the great river, now five miles wide, casts its stupendous volume of water into the Pacific.

East of Portland history and legend combine to lend color to the Oregon towns along the river bank. Cascade Locks, near Bonneville, preserve the past and the legends in a splendid small museum. Where the lock walls now stand, a natural bridge once spanned the river, according to Indian legend. The bridge was cast into the river by Tyhee Sahale, the Supreme Being, angered by his two sons' feud over the beautiful guardian of the bridge's sacred flame. In typical mythological style, the debris created the river's cascades, and the three lovers, who came out second-best in the bridge-hurling spree, were resurrected as Mt. Hood, Mt. Adams, and Mt. St. Helens

Northern
Oregon Coast

Early explorers, such as Captain James Cook and Sir Francis Drake, found the Oregon Coast a rugged and violent introduction to an all-but-empty land. Hundreds of years later much of the Coast is still a solitary place, fascinating and mysterious. Oregon meets the sea along a 400-mile shoreline, from Astoria at its northern limit to Brookings, close to the California border. A relatively small percentage of people around the country are aware of the beauty and variety of Oregon's Coast. The residents seem to prefer it that way, for too many human intruders could steal some of the magic away from "their" Coast with its long, lonely beaches and half-hidden crescent coves stacked with driftwood and beach rocks.

Perhaps nowhere else in the state is the restorative magic of Oregon so pervasive as it is on the Coast. What some of the affluent seek, spending fortunes around the world, is available free for anyone who has the good sense and insight to spend a day or longer just being part of this land-sea ambience. Peace of mind, tranquility, renewal — call it what you will; a feeling of self-forgetfulness and calm is the reward for the solitary beachcomber, the explorer of tide pools, rocks, and lonely stands of coast pine and spruce.

U.S. Highway 101 skirts the shoreline for much of the way, and those who prefer quick glimpses and changes of mood will find a fascinating kaleidoscope of scenic variety as they drive along the winding road. The highway sometimes ventures a few miles farther inland, offering views of coastal flora such as rhododendron, azalea, and salal. Each town has its unique qualities, readily revealed by the residents to visitors who show an interest. The northern coastline contains the more developed or more "commercial" stretches, such as those at Seaside, Cannon Beach, Lincoln City, Depoe Bay, and Newport. It's safe to say that in midsummer one can stake a claim to a large stretch of unoccupied beach or go sightseeing along the bays and boat basins without stepping on the heels of other people doing the same thing.

For the person who feels he must "do" something wherever he goes, towns on the northern coast offer many activities. At Astoria fishing is a big attraction and history is a long suit. The visitor can explore the city's past in a museum or watch, from the hilly site of the Astor Column, giant freighters heading up the Columbia or gliding seaward under the five-mile-long Astoria's Megler Bridge. Seaside, south of Astoria, has a fine swimming beach, in the manner of some of the East Coast ocean resorts, and Oregon's version of a carnival atmosphere. Cannon Beach has a popular bathing beach, with Haystack Rock standing a little out to sea; there's also an artists' colony there, where one can browse and discover interesting uses for driftwood and rock treasures picked up while beachcombing.

The shore turns wilder after Cannon Beach, with capes and points now defining the land-sea border. South of Arch Cape the "Tillamook" stretch of coast begins. It has a special aura for a number of reasons. One of the obvious ones is big, deepwater Tillamook Bay, where bottom and salmon fishing are highly rewarding activities. The bay has some charming communities around or near its shores, like Garibaldi, Manhattan Beach, Rockaway, and Barview. Oswald West State Park is located in this coastal segment. It is like many of the other coastal parks in seeming big and beautiful, but unlike all the others in being a nearly complete wilderness from which motor vehicles are banned. It possesses lush, semi-tropical rain-forest flora to a degree that is unusual even on a coastline where similar shapes are many times repeated.

Mountains meet the sea in many places on the Oregon coast, forming capes and headlands that make this shoreline one of the world's most scenic. Nowhere is this better illustrated than in the remote "Three Capes" area. The coast highway doesn't go there, but connecting roads near the town of Tillamook do. The three capes are different from each other in size and aspect, but all are entitled to the descriptive, "spectacular." Cape Kiwanda, the southernmost one, guards a fine fishing cove from stormy seas; Cape Mears, on the north near Tillamook Bay, has its Octopus Tree; Cape Lookout, in the middle, is an immense basalt headland two miles long and a great attraction for artists and photographers. From Mears to Kiwanda the distance is about 20 miles.

Lincoln City, farther down the Coast, is very visitor-oriented and has been integrated with a string of smaller communities into what is called, in the chamber-of-commerce idiom, the "20 Miracle Miles." Depoe Bay has a thriving charter-boat business for those who like deep-sea fishing and a spectacular scenic loop road for an impressive perspective of the Pacific. At Newport, although many activities beckon the visitor, the pace is slow and inviting, especially on the Yaquina Bay waterfront where the fishermen gather.

Moving down the coast past the charming villages of Waldport and Yachats, the highway climbs high on the shoulders of Cape Perpetua, a massive and lofty rock cliff rising abruptly out of the sea. From the top of the Cape, where a side road leads, the view to the north and south is one of the best in the whole stretch of shoreline. Cape Perpetua also has a Visitor Center with trails leading from it through the tide pool and plant areas of the Cape, where visitors may stroll, study the marine and plant life, and learn about the geological history of the area.

Heceta Head and its lighthouse, next prominent feature of the Cape area, is one of the most photographed places on the Coast. It and the Devil's Churn are but a short distance from Sea Lion Caves, where the visitor can stand on a windy cliff and watch thousands of sea lions taking the sun far below, or he can descend into the interior of the Caves via elevator for an intimate look at the interior of the cavern, which serves the wild sea lions as a year-round home. Mention of sea lions brings to mind the growing population of sea otters all along the Coast. These creatures, once nearly exterminated, are now increasing at a healthy pace, testimony to the effectiveness of Oregon's measures to protect endangered species.

Florence, at about the mid-point on the Coast, is another town that welcomes the visitor but doesn't smother him with this-to-buy and that-to-do. It has an old town section worth exploring.

Southern
Oregon Coast

Those strange, sandy phenomena of nature, the Oregon Dunes, begin just south of Florence and are certainly the dominant feature of the southern half of the Coast for the 45 miles that they stretch toward Coos Bay. The dunes are usually enormous, rolling and rising to heights of more than 250 feet. One would logically conclude that masses of sand of such girth would also be quite substantial, but their contours are continually changing, with the wind acting as a tireless sculptor. A huge dune seen one week may be a deep sand canyon the next, or appear to have lent its mass to a neighboring monster. The Oregon Dunes National Recreation Area marks out the most stupendous works of the windy carver in sand. This is a part of Oregon's coast that lays valid claim to the term, "unique." And if the visitor is not content just to be in the midst of this undulating "Sahara by the Sea," (so-called in a State Highway Department travel promotion), he can ride the stark, roller-coaster landscape in a dune buggy.

Along with the giant sand dunes, this coastal stretch is lavishly endowed with forests and fresh-water lakes and streams, so that in some places one may actually dip one foot in the salty ocean while letting the cool fresh water of a rivulet course between the toes of his other foot. Honeyman State Park, three miles below Florence, has this kind of variety within its borders. The park's environments of lake, woods, and dunes get along very well together. Some 16 more lakes between Florence and North Bend are favorite fishing and camping spots.

Reedsport, another pleasant coast town, is about halfway between Florence and Coos Bay. It is the western terminus of the Umpqua, one of Oregon's more placid rivers, at least along its lower stretches. The Umpqua rises

Heceta Head Lighthouse

Still Creek, Mt. Hood National Forest

Crater Lake

Succor Creek, North of Jordan Valley

Looking South from Neahkahnie Mountain

Silver Falls State Park

Wallowa Mountains

Multnomah Falls

Mt. Hood reflected in Trillium Lake

Near Cape Sebastian

Wallowa Lake

Smith Rocks State Park

Camp Sherman and Metolius River

Columbia Gorge

Tumalo Falls

Yaquina Head Lighthouse

Mt. Hood National Forest

Rock Creek near Dayville

Cape Blanco

Elowah Falls

Battle Rock State Park

Vidae Falls, Crater Lake National Forest

Paulina Peak and Little Crater Lake

Mt. Thielsen and Diamond Lake

Indian Beach

Painted Hills

Historic Jacksonville

Sunset Beach

Prairie Creek and the Wallowa Mountains

Columbia River near Mosier

International Rose Test Gardens, Portland

State Capitol Building, Salem

Mt. Washington and Big Lake

Row River, South Willamette Valley

Portland

Central Oregon near Warm Springs

Fish Lake and Mt. McLoughlin

Upper Rogue River

Mt. Bachelor and Elk Lake

Cape Meares

North and Middle Sisters Mountain from Scott Lake

Timberline Lodge and Mount Hood

Chetco River

Willamette Valley from Mt. Angel

Deep Creek, East of Lakeview

Mt. Jefferson

Sahalie Falls

Broken Top Mountain and Sparks Lake

in the Cascades and pursues a meandering course west and northwest through the Coast Range. If one follows it from the valley town of Drain along an easy, broad road to the Coast, he can partake of no more sumptuous riverine beauty anywhere. Coos Bay, a little way down the line (with its partner city, North Bend), is the premier lumber shipping port of the world. It can also be boastful about its striped bass fishing. South of this town are four of the 32 coastal state parks along the long coastline. The four parks — Sunset Beach, Shore Acres, Cape Arago, and Bullards Beach — are in settings of extraordinary beauty.

This stretch begins the wildest and loneliest part of the coastline. One can drive the 40-odd miles from Coos Bay to Cape Blanco and Port Orford with little for company except sea, sand, sky, and the highway. There are some towns along the way, but they are only minor interruptions in the general solitude of the seascape and landscape. Cape Blanco is the westernmost point in Oregon. It has a picturesque lighthouse, and its setting is another example of the magnificence that is characteristic of the Coast.

The southern Coast has its own private and separate peak — Humbug Mountain, six miles below Battle Rock. This 1,750-foot-high eminence is also a state park and a beach. Here the persevering beachcomber may find all sorts of riches yielded by the sea; treasures, such as Japanese glass floats, bottles, marine fossils, jasper, petrified wood, bamboo, kegs, and driftwood.

Pushing on the 28 miles to Gold Beach, one is getting close to the California border. Gold Beach has become known as the place to make those 32-mile trips up the untamed Rogue River to Agness. Every day mail boats leave the Wedderburn dock just north of Gold Beach for the 64-mile round-trip, taking on tourists for the thrilling run by jet-powered boat. South of Gold Beach the scenery is just as showy, and before arriving at Brookings on the border, the traveler may be moved to gape at the colossal rock formations rising from the sea, at the wild flowers growing from dunes, or at the sweeping undulations of the coastal countryside. The *piece de resistance* is at Brookings, where Azalea State Park, named for its sprawling acres of azaleas, offers an idyllic setting for a rest and a meal, with wild cherries, butterflies, and hummingbirds for company.

Willamette Valley

Picture one of the richest agricultural areas anywhere, a broad swath of land that stretches eastward to the high Cascades and west to the Coast Range. At the north end is Portland and at the south, Eugene. In this fertile region — the Willamette Valley — lives the major part of Oregon's population. The Willamette River, on or near whose banks much of the state's history was made, winds through the valley from south to north. In former days the river was used as the only means of transportation, until the railroads took over that task in the 1870s.

The three biggest Oregon cities — including Salem and the two mentioned previously, Eugene and Portland — are situated along the river. But a smaller town than these can claim more historical glory. This is Oregon City, just south of Portland. It was the first incorporated town west of the Mississippi and the territorial seat of government before Oregon became a state. Oregon City is rather a retiring sort of town, so few people — even Oregonians — are fully appreciative of its historical importance. The city's founder, Dr. John McLoughlin, figured prominently in the western operations of the Hudson's Bay Company. Today his house is a national historic site. There are also other buildings that are reminders of Oregon City's — and Oregon's — past, and two historic burial grounds.

South from Oregon City, near the geographical center of the Willamette Valley, is Salem, the capital. Theodore Winthrop, the mid-nineteenth century traveler in the Northwest, described Salem as "a village on one of those exquisite plains . . . where the original oak trees have been left about." Many of the murals and sculptures of the State Capitol are based on themes concerned with the Lewis and Clark expedition. Salem is a calm, quiet place for a city of its size and importance. One of the important things it does every year is play host to the Oregon State Fair in late summer, when the myriad products of the fertile Willamette farmland are symbolized in carefully arranged exhibits. The Willamette River in the general-Salem area has a special picturesque side in three back-country free ferries; one near Canby, the Wheatland ferry between Newberg and Salem, and the Buena Vista ferry northwest of Albany. All three ferry crossings have strong links to the nineteenth century in Oregon.

About 50 miles east of Salem is Detroit Dam, one of man's more successful manipulations of raw nature. The dam backs up the North Santiam River for eight-and-a-half miles, creating Detroit Lake, and creates an out-of-character tranquility for the normally impetuous river that flashes down from the Mt. Jefferson Wilderness. The narrow canyon where the dam restrains the rivers has a fairyland quality about it. Standing on the ramparts of the dam, one sees in one direction the lovely blue lake reflecting, jewel-like, the perfection of its setting; on the other side, looking down as from the prow of a ship, one can see far below on the canyon floor the leaping, dancing river rejoicing in being free once more of constraints. The mists sent up the canyon walls by the churning water add to the dream-like feeling.

At the southern terminus of the Willamette Valley, Eugene sits astride the river like some very authoritative matron intent on meeting all travelers before they are allowed to pass on their way. The image may be a little strained, but here, where the mountains start to pinch off the valley, one is almost driven into the arms of this lumbering capital of 108,000-plus people. But that's not so bad. Eugene is a friendly place. Add to this the hard-to-find mixture of rural beauty and metropolitan sophistication, and a picture of an attractive community emerges.

Willamette Valley

to Rogue River Country

From Eugene south to Grants Pass, about 138 miles, the terrain offers great variety, including wooded mountainsides, flashing rivers, and isolated valleys. It's a colorful historical area as well. Throughout the Bohemia Mining District southeast of Cottage Grove are reminders of gold mining, including the Bohemia Gold Mining Days celebration in July. Many of the mines are still in existence and may be visited during summer and autumn in self-guided tours. The District is named for "Bohemia" Johnson, who discovered gold in 1863 while he was supposedly hiding out in the Calapooya Mountains. Before long a hundred claims were staked out and the Bohemia Mining District was created. Other metals in addition to gold were found, but no great riches were dug out of the Bohemia. Now the charm of this part of Oregon is in the mining relics, the incredibly long views from the mountains round about, the wildlife, the racing mountain streams, and the dark gorges with their sharply sloping walls.

Just south of Cottage Grove, if one is driving along the north-south freeway, he has a chance to do some pleasant, easy exploring by car. At this point Highway 99 leaves the big Interstate 5 and takes off through the small lumbering towns of Drain, Yoncalla, Oakland, Sutherlin, Wilbur, Winchester, Winston, Dillard and Myrtle Creek. Roseburg is in their midst, but since it is a "big" town, it is served by the freeway. From Roseburg one may visit the fascinating little country town of Lookingglass, 10 miles west, where the only parking meter is in front of the general store.

The town of Drain is a key to Highway 38, which heads for the sea along the graceful lower Umpqua River, a stretch of waterway mentioned elsewhere in this book. But that isn't the whole story of the Umpqua. The lower Umpqua, which meanders to the Pacific, is but a short segment of the squiggly thread of a river that finds its way through the hills north of Roseburg, after a journey from the high Cascades, as the North Umpqua River. The North Umpqua is paralleled faithfully by Oregon Highway 138, but drivers usually miss the best parts of a trip like this. It would be nice to have a pair of snap-on helicopter blades when moseying along the North Umpqua valley, because this is country meant for hovering and looking. The river shows many faces along this part of its length, and its moods range from calm, through wild, to savage. There are some odd rock chimneys and natural arches to stare at when you reach Dry Creek, 10 miles east of the town of Steamboat, as well as in Indian Cave with pictographs on the walls.

Roseburg to Grants Pass is full of great scenery, but a lot of it is found around communities that are reached only by side trips from the main highway. In Wolf Creek there's a big slice of history, as well. Wolf Creek Tavern is supposed to have sheltered, for a time, Ulysses S. Grant, when he was a second lieutenant touring the West. Other notables believed to have partaken of the inn's hospitality are General Sherman, Joaquin Miller, and even Jack London. Wolf Creek Road, starting near the tavern, is an adventurous way to get to Grants Pass. It brushes by old gold mines, backcountry settlements, and the glamorous Rogue River, itself. At Grants Pass, the visitor has the opportunity to take full advantage of the Rogue. There are river-boat excursions that truly show the beauty of the Rogue and offer an exciting and exhilarating experience.

Central Oregon

Central Oregon is a kind of buffer between the lush vegetation and thick forests of the western slopes and the arid, open desert vistas of Eastern Oregon. It partakes of attributes of both regions and, in its own way, merits superlatives as extravagant as those used to portray the other areas. For the summer tourist, it possesses all the marvelous attributes that travel agents are wont to endow places with — "outdoor paradise," "crystal clear lakes abundant with trout," "magnificent scenic vistas." The city of Bend is, generally, considered the hub of the region. It is located at the middle of the north-south line. And it is the natural starting point for excursions into high mountains and ski slopes, for sorties into forests of jackpine and stands of Ponderosa. Or for a change of pace, you can ramble along the high valley floor, where random growths of sage punctuate the open rangeland, reminding the traveler that to the east is a harsher clime and a thirstier land.

Bend, on the Deschutes River, is famous as a clean-looking, attractive resort and year-round-living town. Its sparkling looks, unbelievably clear, dry air (its elevation is 3,600 feet), and moderate climate make it a comfortable place to settle in. Century Drive, a well-known scenic route, begins and ends in Bend. Formally called Cascade Lakes Highway, the route forms a rough square, one segment of which soars 3,000 feet from Bend up into the heart of the Cascades. Along its 100-mile length, when not flirting with Bachelor Butte and some of the other handsome spires of the central Cascades, the road slices through Deschutes National Forest, rides over black lava flows, and passes cinder cones and obsidian cliffs. It crosses mountain meadows full of sweet-smelling wildflowers and touches near Forest Service campgrounds, primitive areas, and lakes, one of which — Elk — is a starting point for pack trains into the Three Sisters Wilderness. Hardly a sign of civilization disturbs the natural serenity of the scene until the road finally curves back to U.S. 97 for the final leg back to Bend. This part of the road touches turnoffs to lakes, craters, a lava forest, resort and recreation areas, a volcanic site, and lava and ice caves.

The scenic variety compressed into the comparatively few miles of Century Drive would make Central Oregon sufficient unto itself, if that were the whole story. But anyone who has been north to Redmond, Prineville, Madras, and the Warm Springs Indian Reservation with its Indian-operated resort, Kah-Nee-Ta, would be loath to leave out these contributors to the area's attractions. Prineville, 15 miles east of Redmond, leads into the beautiful Ochoco Mountains. Nearby are the Ochoco and Prineville reservoirs, and east of the mountains is a small but fascinating area called the Painted Hills, whose barren landscape of treeless mounds and gullies is thought to have been created in the distant past by volcanic activity in the Cascades. The striated coloration of the hills increases the eerie unreality of the place.

A few miles north of Redmond the north-south highway (U.S. 97) passes over the Crooked River Gorge, a deep, sheer-sided canyon carved by the river, still carving far below in the canyon floor as it twists on its serpentine course. To the north on the same road is Madras, an agricultural center. Northwest of Madras is the Warm Springs Indian Reservation and the elegant spa, Kah-Nee-Ta. This region of high plateaus, giant natural sculpture, and awesome coloring stirs memories of many a story of the Old West and the harsh lives endured by the early inhabitants.

The Mountains

Oregon's Cascade Range dominates the state's mountain environment, because the range's height and unbroken line from north to south makes it a major regulating factor in the state's weather. And the timbered wealth of these mountains gives them first place in Oregon's economy. The Cascades are almost-extinct volcanoes. The "almost" lends excitement to their character. Volcanism is said to have begun in the Cascades about 10-million years ago and is still showing some limited activity. In 1980 Mt. St. Helens, located south of Mt. Rainier in Washington State, just north of Portland and part of the Cascade Range, became over zealous and popped its top and north side all to pieces. Since that time there have been occasional explosions. However, activity has been minor for several years, now. Mt. Hood, Mt. Rainier, and some of the other Cascade peaks have vents from which steam issues.

The dramatic beauty of the Cascade peaks is nowhere more apparent than in the Central Cascades. Here the Mt. Jefferson Wilderness Area sets off the rugged, snowy peak that rises more than 10,000 feet. Jefferson Park below the mountain is a favorite spot for hikers and nature lovers because of its alpine meadows, its wildflowers, and its streams and lakes. Farther south, about 70 miles due east of Eugene, are the Three Sisters — North, Middle, and South — all over 10,000 feet. They also have their own wilderness area, but hiking to them is not necessary to get a "close-up" look. The McKenzie Pass from Eugene provides motorists a spectacular view at close range of these beauties, as well as sights of other peaks far away to the north and south. The Pass, itself, takes second place to none of the Cascades' scenic delights. For some 50 miles it parallels the McKenzie River, one of the most glamorous recreational streams in the West. Then in the area of its summit, the Pass shows off a jumble of black lava, one of the most impressive flows in the United States.

South of the Three Sisters, and reached by side roads off Highway 58 from Eugene, is a group of high mountain lakes and reservoirs of great beauty. One of these is Waldo Lake, the second largest natural lake in Oregon. The U.S. Forest Service has taken great pains to preserve the beautiful alpine aspect of this lake. Some of the other lakes in this mountain area, the first two of which are accessible from Highway 58, are Odell, Crescent, Davis, and Cultus.

To the north and south of the Central Cascades are a number of mountain landmarks of distinctive grandeur, the most notable and obvious being Mt. Hood, the monarch of Oregon mountains. Hood is a much-climbed and visited mountain and a popular skiing area on its lower reaches. But its proximity to Portland and accessibility via trails and settlements on its approaches do not diminish its hypnotic fascination for anyone who gazes at it. Hood is visible from almost any high point in the state, but one of the most magical views of the mountain is from the western hills of Portland, where it seems to float lightly just above the eastern skyline. Man has paid tribute to this magic mountain by building on its flank a ski lodge of gargantuan proportions and ornate art — Timberline Lodge. The Lodge was completed in 1937 as a project of the Works Progress Administration and stands as the expression of the work of many artisans.

The southern Cascades have their fair share of impressive and towering peaks: Diamond Peak, Mt. Scott, Mt. Thielsen, Mt. McLoughlin. And there are a few areas reserved for wilderness. West and south of Odell Lake is the Diamond Peak Wilderness, easily accessible, like the Three Sisters Wilderness to the north. In contrast to this is the Mountain Lakes Wilderness northwest of Klamath Falls. This relatively unknown area is part of the Winema National Forest. Because most of the Wilderness is above the 6,000-foot-level, trails are often blocked until late June by heavy snows.

Southern Oregon

The loose regional label, "Southern Oregon," is hard-pressed to cover all of the vast area that makes up the southern part of the state. Part of the problem is the way Oregonians think about their state. In the west the Umpqua and Rogue valleys are considered as very much separate from the Southern Oregon that forms the Crater Lake and Klamath Falls areas to the east, and certainly not in the least identifiable with Southeastern Oregon. The narrow valleys of the southern Cascades and Siskiyous are more "west" than south, having greater affinities with the Willamette Valley to the north than with any other area.

The western portion of southern Oregon is a region whose topography and climate mark it as a transitional area between the damp west and drier east. It is a combination of dry chaparral, gold and green rolling hills, and green forests similar to the thick fir stands characteristic of more northerly parts of the state. The biggest town in this varied region is Medford, center of a lush orchard country whose plentiful water, fertile lands, and long, warm summers produce pears, peaches and other fruit of a quality unsurpassed anywhere. Medford is also the center of a thriving resort area, drawing large numbers of retired persons, who are attracted by its dry air, lakes, many fishing streams, and natural beauty.

Just a few miles west of Medford is Jacksonville, which still projects the excitement of the gold-rush days. The old county courthouse is now a museum, and many of the buildings and homes, with their turrets, gables, and intricate woodwork, have been preserved to maintain their nineteenth-century character. In August the Peter Britt Music Festival is held here.

Ashland, south of Medford, is a contrast to the mining towns of the Rogue area. For many years it has been known before all else as the home of the celebrated Oregon Shakespearean Festival, launched in 1935 by Angus Bowmer, a member of the Southern Oregon College faculty. Performances are given in beautiful Lithia Park, designed by John McLaren, the creator of San Francisco's Golden Gate Park. Mt. Ashland, 7,523 feet high, dominates this exquisite setting, with its outdoor and indoor theatres, placed alongside a little jewel of a lake in the park.

Let us now consider the south-central and southeastern regions, from Klamath Falls east to the border. About 60 miles north of Klamath Falls lies one of the most glamorous and mystical ornaments in the Cascade diadem. Crater Lake, whose indescribable beauty has evoked more description than any other single geological feature of Oregon, still defies the limited power of words to convey the full range of its magic. One of nature's colossal rearrangements of her decor, Crater Lake was formed from the explosion and collapse of Mt. Mazama, when the shell of the volcano gradually filled with rain. The lake is the deepest on the continent (more than 2,000 feet), about 20 square miles in area, and with two islands whose names, Wizard and Phantom Ship, tell much about the effect of the area on those who visit it.

Within a short range of Klamath Falls are many and varied natural attractions. Lake of the Woods, about 30 miles away, is guarded by 9,495-foot Mt. McLoughlin. And Upper Klamath National Wildlife Refuge, a sanctuary for waterfowl, is even closer. Collier Memorial State Park, 30 miles north, contains logging equipment used in earlier times and reconstructed loggers' shacks. Within the park Spring Creek and Williamson River make their contributions to the idyllic scenery, and the nearby Sprague River beckons sports fishermen. Chiloquin, three miles south, displays Indian regional history in its Klamath Indian Memorial Museum. Not to neglect the obvious, huge Upper Klamath Lake is never very far away. Klamath Falls is at the southern tip, and roads skirt the east and west shores of the stretched-out lake. Some of the area's pelicans stay at Lake Ewauna in downtown Klamath Falls, apparently preferring a taste of city life. To the south and east of Klamath Falls, the villages of Merrill, Malin, and Bonanza are picturesque examples of Oregon's rural communities.

History is part of the daily life of Klamath Falls. There are buildings still in use, like the Baldwin Hotel, which have an appearance and an aura relating them to the past. Several museums containing artifacts of western history and art give our emotional link with history a constant infusion of strength.

A long hop to the east, almost 100 miles by road, is Lakeview, almost in the middle of southern Oregon, and the highest, at 4,800 feet of any town in the state. Although it is still a marketing town for large cattle spreads in the area, the days of great herds and roundups are over. Lakeview has become a headquarters for tourist forays into the region's desert country, unspoiled lakes, and other scenic attractions. One of these attractions just beyond the edge of town, is "Old Perpetual," the only continuously spouting geyser in the United States, shooting its steaming column of water 60 feet into the air. Fifteen miles south there's Goose Lake, which extends halfway into California. To the west, beyond Quartz Mountain Pass, the Gearhart Mountain Wilderness is a refuge for large animal populations.

About 20 miles north of Lakeview, Abert Lake mirrors the desert alongside U.S. Highway 395. On the eastern lake edge, Abert Rim, a giant fault scarp, pushes with a startling abruptness 2,000 feet above the plateau. From the summit of this sheer precipice, the simmering vision of desolate plains and hills is an indelible experience.

Still farther north, on Oregon Highway 31, are Paisley, a former cattle town, and Summer Lake, whose waters are strongly alkaline and, in some years, scarce. As Oregon 31 continues on north and west, it passes the wide plains and low hills of Fort Rock Valley, whose caves have revealed much evidence of the human hunting and fishing cultures of 10,000 and more years ago.

Northeast of Lakeview is the magnificent and unique Hart Mountain National Antelope Refuge. Antelope, mule deer, bighorn sheep, and many other species are protected on this volcanic massif, which reaches 3,000 feet above the plain. The Refuge area is a complete ecological universe. Its zones range from hot semi-desert to snowy mountain, and the Warner Lakes grouping to the west is home for hundreds of thousands of birds. The explorer of the Hart Mountain area will find rough roads and few comforts, but much unspoiled landscape.

When one traces with his finger on a map of southeastern Oregon, he can find scant evidence of man's incursions. Oregon Highway 140 takes off east from a few miles north of Lakeview, and it passes only one village in Oregon before dipping down into Nevada on its 102-mile journey to Denio. What remains to the east are the Steens Mountains, U.S. Highway 95 slashing north-south through the mountains and prairies, the upper Owyhee River and its canyon, and a lot of empty land in between. Near the border, but more northerly than Lakeview's latitude, the Owyhee hills spread out in the sun to the north of Jordan Valley on the eastern border. This is Oregon's Basque country or former Basque country, for even this mostly man-forsaken area has been Americanized and homogenized. The Basque herders with their thousands of sheep covering the Owyhee hills are gone. The original Basques from the Pyrenees are retired, have passed on, or are doing other things. Their music and speech, once predominant in Jordan Valley, are rarely heard, although the old-timers sometimes get together to speak the mother tongue.

One constant of this region has been its isolation from the rest of Oregon. Jordan Valley, whose population is now about 200, is farther from the nearest sizeable settlement than any other Oregon town. It is still a very colorful place all through its rather limited extent. Some of its buildings are eloquent witness to the early part of this century. Built of native stone, they include a church, a hotel (abandoned), and a general store with a wooden sidewalk.

West of the Steens, back across the barren land, is the town of Frenchglen. Its population of 20 or so makes it a good-sized settlement for this part of Oregon. The town's strongly frontier-style hotel is worth a long look. Its rough-hewn lobby serves as a gathering place in the evenings for the few human beings around.

Eastern Oregon

Sometimes a regional label turns out to be a less-than-perfect designation for an area. Here and there some of the landscape oozes into territory that people have classified, for their convenience, as something else. Eastern Oregon is like this. Its natural western border might be considered the Deschutes River which flows from below Bend north to the Columbia, but the Central Oregon people claim identification with a lot of that area. Its southern stretches blend into the desolate reaches of southeastern Oregon. But no matter if they're a little hazy around the edges, the eastern lands have a flavor that's distinctive enough to give the visitor a sense of where he is.

Some people think they're in Eastern Oregon at The Dalles. It's a good starting point because of its place in history, for here is where the Oregon Trail finally jumped the Cascades (in 1845). The trail that cuts over the mountains to Oregon City was named the Barlow Road, in honor of the man who made it possible.

Some of the "real" east of Oregon is the country around Pendleton, still in the north but 130-miles deeper into the east. Pendleton is the largest town in Eastern Oregon and, of course, is home of the famous Round-up, held every September. Rodeo cowboys come from all over the country to compete, and many tribes are represented by hundreds of Indian performers. Just east of Pendleton is the Umatilla Indian Reservation, where the reservation road follows the old Oregon Trail for several miles. A little farther on is Bingham Springs on the edge of the Blue Mountains, and the freeway (84N) follows the Oregon Trail southeast to La Grande.

La Grande and its environs are worth a long pause. To the north lies the perfectly flat Grande Ronde Valley, a fascinating panorama of lush farms that can be seen in one sweep of the eye from vantage points on nearby heights. The past and present are next-door neighbors here: North Powder, to the south, reminds one of the stagecoach era; 20 miles to the west is Anthony Lakes, a sparkling recreation area perched 7,000 feet up in the Blue Mountains' Elkhorn Range. Imbler, a few miles north of La Grande, possesses some reminders of the late nineteenth century. The town of Cove to the east sits on the edge of the Grande Ronde Valley, where the Wallowas proclaim their dominion.

The configurations of the Wallowas remind the visitor of Alpine settings — the region is often called the "Switzerland of America." The wilderness at the heart of the Wallowas goes by the name "Wallowa Wonderland." Wallowa Lake, the largest of 60 lakes in these mountains, is south of the "cow town" of Joseph, close to the eastern border. The lake reflects the snow-covered Wallowa peaks, some of which tower more than 10,000 feet over it. The tallest and most impressive are Sacajawea Peak and the Matterhorn, a near replica of the other Matterhorn. Pack trains are available for exploring the Eagle Cap Wilderness of the Wallowas. Or, the visitor may ride the aerial tramway that soars up from the 4,000-foot level of the nearby lake to the top of 8,000-foot Mt. Howard. To the east and south is the historic town of Oxbow, then Oxbow Dam, holding back the savage Snake River, with the help of Hell's Canyon to the north and Brownlee to the south.

Bending around to the west, the traveler comes to Baker, once the center of Oregon's gold country. The mining camps lived only briefly, leaving a few tumbledown cabins as testimony to their existence. Sumpter, 26 miles west, was the largest of the mining towns. It had 3,000 residents in the 1890s. Now it has about 150. The scenery in this valley is superb, even if the gold mines were not. But the ghost towns that were once centers of mining activity are now lending their picturesque remains to the decor around Baker.

The John Day country to the west, sandwiched within the Malheur National Forest, has its particular sense of history. The famous fossil beds in this region record geological history of millions of years, dating back to the time when most of Oregon was covered by the sea. John Day, itself, is a legendary cattle town where, up to a few years ago, massive cattle drives were conducted down Main Street. The proximity of the Strawberry Range of the Blue Mountains and the bright meadowland around the town give it an appearance of rugged beauty. Another reminder of the wild west era in this part of Oregon is nearby Canyon City, rich with history of the gold rush days. Canyon City is also the home of Joaquin Miller, the "Poet of the Sierra," whose cabin is on the grounds of a historical museum. In its heyday Canyon City had a population of more than 10,000. Now it has about 700 inhabitants. Burns, some 70 miles due south of John Day, was once the center of a great cattle empire, and more great names in cattle ranching are associated with it than with any other place in Oregon.